HELLO, PRIESTHOOD, GOODBYE

by

Christian A. Semeniano

TABLE OF CONTENTS

CHAPTER ONE

Unveiling the truth

Currently, one of the issues that the Roman Catholic Church faces involves priestly departure. From 1964 to 2004, there were 69,063 priests who left the priesthood (Schutz, 2007). Between 1975 and 2008, the Catholics all over the world have increased by 64% from 709.6 million to 1.166 billion; however, the number of priests increased by only 1% from 404,783 to 409,166 (Center for Applied Research in the Apostolate, n.d). Consequently, in a period where priests are needed most, gradually concerns the Catholic Church.

Leaving the priesthood is a matter of decision-making in which priests experience "struggle of faith, personal commitment, and the dark night of the soul" (Hickson & Gudz, 1995, p. 5). It is also considered as a long process of searching for one's soul (Rice, as cited in Hickson & Gudz, 1995). Moreover, priests who left experience a number of injustices, isolation, confusion, and anxiety (Catholic Answers Staff, 2016). According to Fernandez (2001), although there are a lot of factors that affect priestly departure, people usually think that being involved with a woman is the primary reason.

All priests undergo spiritual formation before being ordained. Their formation consists of a long and difficult preparation (Fernandez, 2001) which includes a discernment process to know what God desires for them (Hankle, 2010). The seminary formation consists of almost twelve to thirteen years depending on the type of priesthood, whether secular/diocesan or religious. According to Fernandez (2001), a secular or diocesan priest is ordained for the purpose of serving a specific diocese, on the other hand, a religious priest belongs to a religious order or congregation; however, not all members of this congregation are ordained priests. Some are ordained simply as 'brothers'. Each type of priest has its own distinct procedures and processes of priestly formation.

Aspirants to the priesthood usually spend four years in a minor seminary, which entails four years of philosophical training, and four to five years of theological studies. They are typically allowed to take a break from the seminary at least once a month to visit their families. Then, they can spend a longer period of time with their families during semestral, Christmas, and summer breaks (Fernandez, 2001).

Kennedy and Heckler (as cited in Hickson & Gudz, 1995) argued that the process of priestly formation hinders the normal psychological growth and development of the aspirants. They noted that, "Seminary formation did, after all, reward conformity, a certain passivity to regulation and authority as well as a willingness to stay away from many normal developmental experiences such as dating and a normal life" (p. 7). Indeed, aspiring priests are usually deprived of the things that some Psychologists believe are important for the normal development of a person such as opposite-sex friendship, romance, home environment, parties, dances, proms, social media friends, and even mobile phones and gadgets (Fernandez, 2001).

Pietkiewicz and Bachryj (as cited in Pietkiewicz, 2016) reported that priesthood has a particular lifestyle. A priest possesses an image of the valued spiritual leader, usually seen as a lifelong calling (Isacco et al., 2014). He assumes this leadership role right after his ordination in which he professes three solemn vows: obedience, celibacy, and poverty (Fernandez, 2001). Obedience refers to the promise of a priest to obey his Bishop at most. Therefore, the Bishop has the power and authority over him. The second is, celibacy which refers to the promise of abstaining from sex and carnal pleasures. Lastly, poverty which refers to "detachment from worldly possessions coupled with a spirit of trust in God" (Acts and Decrees of the Second Plenary Council of the Philippines, no. 584). He is also called to renounce personal ambitions and decision making (Schoenherr & Young, 1993). After ordination to the priesthood, he usually starts as assistant priest of the parish for around five years and then, can be transferred to another parish as decided by his Bishop (Fernandez, 2001).

Despite long years of formation, a priest could experience vocational crisis (Fernandez, 2001; Umoren, 2006). This crisis is a state of conflict that may be internal or external, leading to the experience of meaninglessness and powerlessness. It is internal when the intrapsychic dynamics of the priest such as interaction among needs, attitudes, and values are disorganized and disoriented. On the other hand, it is external when it is triggered by external factors such as community, family, and other social factors. Consequently, a priest might experience vocational crisis that may lead to priestly departure (Umoren, 2006).

Leaving the priesthood has a long and difficult process; it involves a laicization or dispensation procedure that can take years. This procedure frees a priest of his powers, rights, and authority to administer the Sacraments (Catholic Answers Staff, 2016). He is also freed from the discipline of celibacy and is allowed to get married (Pope, 2015).

In the Philippines, commitment to the priesthood has been shown to be affected by personal, organizational, and cultural factors. According to Fernandez (2001), these factors challenged the common perception that romantic involvement with women is the main reason. Aside from these, Cornelio (2012) found that economic limitation, problems with their Bishop, and relational isolation are additional challenges of the priesthood; these factors may affect the decision of a priest to stay in or leave the priesthood at any particular stage of his life (Fernandez, 2001; Sunardi, 2014).

CHAPTER TWO

Brief History of Priestly Departure

Leaving the priesthood is a late twentieth-century phenomenon. Hickson and Gudz (1995) reported that more than 100,000 priests in the Catholic Church have left the priesthood after the Second Vatican Council (1962-1965). From 1914 to 1962, 810 requests for laicization or dispensation were submitted to the Vatican. For this request, 315 were approved while 495 were rejected. From 1964 to 1988, there were 44,890 requests and 39,149 were approved. However, 5,741 requests for dispensation were denied. In total, 39,464 dispensation were granted and 6,236 rejected out of 45,700 requests were sent to the Vatican. On the other hand, from 1970 up to 2004, 11,213 priests decided to return to the priesthood (Schutz, 2007). According to Rakosza (2016), the document released by the Vatican in 2007 reported that there was an average of 1,076 priests who left the priesthood between the years 2000 and 2004.

In Italy, a growing number of priests asking for dispensation arose between 1976 and 1977.There were between 8,000 to 10,000 priests who left the priesthood to marry. Conversely, from 1970 to 1995, 46,000 priests left but not for marriage while in 1998, 618 more priests left the priesthood. Today, between 500 and 700 requests for dispensation have been granted every year (Vatican Insider, 2014).

This phenomenon of priestly departure has not been duly examined in the Philippines. According to Guerrero (as cited in Fernandez, 2001), what has been known in the media were stories of former priests who have decided to leave the priesthood to marry. This shows the common belief that priests leave the priesthood because of a woman. According to official statistics from the Vatican, there are 135 Filipino Bishops, 5,993 secular/diocesan priests, and 2,973 religious priests in the Philippines (Cornelio, 2012). However, according to Catholic

Bishops' Conference in the Philippines (CBCP), there were about 200 Filipino priests who left the priesthood in the last two decades to get married (Fernandez, 2001); but not all of these priestly departures were officially noted (Annuarium Statisticum Ecclesiae, as cited in Fernandez, 2001). In 2004, Archbishop Luis Antonio Cardinal Tagle announced that the Catholic Church needs at least 25,000 priests to serve the 68 million Catholics (Uy, 2013).

According to Sunardi (2014), studies which examined the reasons why priests left the priesthood started in 1930's. One of the findings showed that social factors and the commitment for the priesthood are important for explaining the priestly departure (Verdieck, Shields, & Hoge, 1988). On the other hand, a statistical view of the studies on priestly departure would indicate that most studies have focused on sociological (30%), theological (42%) and psychological (65%) researches (Diekmann; Gautier, Perl, & Fichter; Rossetti, as cited in Sunardi, 2014). Some studies were foreign and conducted by foreign scholars on foreign priests who decided to leave the priesthood. According to Fernandez (2001), the priestly departure of a foreign priest is not necessarily the same with that of a Filipino priest. In addition, a lot of former priests do not want to be called an 'ex-priest' or 'former priest'; instead, they want to be called 'a married priest'.

CHAPTER THREE

Various Reasons of Priestly Departure

In a sociological study of Fernandez (2001), having an affair with a woman is not the only reason why priest leaves his vows. There were still other factors which affected his commitment which in turn led to his departure. Fernandez (2001) proposed three factors of priestly departure: personal-level factors, organizational-level factors, and cultural-level factors. In personal-level factors, a priest decides to leave the priesthood because of factors that border on personal or internal such as identity crisis, midlife crisis, generativity or procreativity, burn-out, quest for inner harmony, buried bomb syndrome, attitudinal flexibility and open-mindedness, and sense of security provided by the existence of a viable alternative-career. These factors do not come from external factors, but rather within the self. The second factor is organizational-level factors such as role uncertainty or ambiguity, role conflict, clerical politics, and lazy monopoly syndrome wherein a priest's decision to leave the priesthood originated from organizational environment. Lastly, cultural-level factors such as Filipino's familial concept of the self, Filipino's collective view of commitment, and Filipino semiology may impel a priest to leave the priesthood.

Kane (as cited in Sunardi, 2014) specified four major reasons for leaving the priesthood: (a) falling in love or desiring a marriage, (b) objecting to celibacy, (c) having problems with authority figures and church administration, and (d) struggling with serious personal or psychological problems. Similarly, Hoge (as cited in Guillen, 2009) found that the most common reasons of priestly departure were the following: (a) falling in love, (b) rejecting celibacy, (c) experiencing disillusion, and (d) feeling rejected as a gay person. He added, "All four types have one condition in common - that the man felt lonely or unappreciated. This is a necessary requirement in the process of deciding to resign; when it is absent, resignation from the priesthood is unlikely" (p. 64). Hickson & Gudz (1995) stated that in order to provide a better understanding about the phenomenon of priestly departure, it is necessary to know the needs, satisfactions, and frustrations of a priest in the priesthood.

Loneliness of the Priestly Life

VandenBos (2006) described loneliness as a matter of emotional and psychological state as well as the lack or absence of companionship or intimacy that resulted from the unfulfilled basic needs of the vocational crisis. Verdiek, Shields, and Hoge (1988) interviewed both resigned and active priests in 1970 and in 1985. They found that those priests who left the priesthood had experienced loneliness and noted that the desire to marry is related to loneliness. Moreover, Louque (2006) stated that loneliness of the priestly life is a common reason of those priests who left the priesthood. Similarly, Hoge and Okure (2006) studied the international priests and found a high level of loneliness and feeling of alienation among them. Adler (as cited in Hickson & Gudz, 1995) theorized that one human need is to belong because it helps develop a healthy personality especially among the priests.

Hoge and Wenger (as cited in Louque, 2006) surveyed 1,279 active priests and found that there are two major sources of satisfaction in the priesthood which include (a) working with others and being part of their lives and (b) being part of the society. However, Arackal (2015) and Umoren (2016) argued that when a priest is affectively immature and experiences bitterness, discontent, and loneliness of the priestly life, he would likely abandon the priestly vocation and may develop a vocational crisis later on. In addition, Pietkiewicz and Bachryj (as cited in Pietkiewicz, 2016) found that one of the challenges that a priest faces in the priesthood is loneliness of the priestly life.

Fernandez (2001) and Rossetti and Rhoades (2013) reported higher levels of psychological distress, burn out, frustration, emotionally drained, and depression among the priests. The study of Knox, Virginia, Thull, and Lombardo (2005) showed that there was a significant relationship between the depression experienced by priests and the low levels of vocational satisfaction in the priesthood; these challenges and difficulties of the priests in the priesthood may lead to priestly departure (Baniak, as cited in Pietkiewicz, 2016).

According to DellaCava (1975) and Umoren (2006), thinking about leaving the priesthood may result in internal conflict of the priests which may lead to priestly departure. However, the nature of the conflict that a priest experiences has not been duly examined from a psychological point of view (DellaCava, 1975) and focused more on a sociological inquiry (Fernandez, 2001).

Desire for an intimate relationship or marriage

Greeley (as cited in Sunardi, 2014) found that the desire for an intimate relationship or marriage is one of the most common reasons of priestly departure; however, this is not always limited to a man and woman relationship (VandenBos, 2006). In the study of Verdieck et al., (1988), they compared two groups of priests in 1970 which consisted of 3,405 priests and in 1985 which consisted of 929 priests. They found that the desire for an intimate relationship or marriage is one of the tendencies among the two groups of priests to leave the priesthood.

Similarly, Greeley (2004) studied two groups of resigned priests in 1970 and in 2000. He also found that the desire for an intimate relationship or marriage is the most common reason for leaving the priesthood. Moreover, Hoge (as cited in Guillen, 2009) reported that 42% of resigned priests left the priesthood because of the desire for an intimate relationship or marriage. In the United States, a former Benedictine monk reported that half of the 53,000 Catholic priests have difficulty in mandatory celibacy. According to Toufexis (as cited in Fernandez, 2001), 28% of these priests are engaged in a relationship with a woman. However, Arackal (2015) argued that there are only few priests who want to fall in love and live with a woman.

In 1991, the Catholic Church of the Philippines stated that there were priests who engaged themselves in a relationship with a woman (Fernandez, 2001). Yana (as cited in Fernandez, 2001) revealed that 4,000 out of 6,000 Catholic priests in the Philippines had a secret relationship, but only 1,000 of them decided to leave the priesthood to marry their partners. However, the Catholic Church of the Philippines reacted to this issue and described it as something 'exaggerated' (Avendano, as cited in Fernandez, 2001).

In a survey, Pietkiewicz (2016) found that most of the priests left the priesthood because of a woman. These former priests reported concerns on how society would react on their departure from priesthood. Consequently, Cornelio (2012) also found through a survey that 68% of the former priests have already thought of leaving the priesthood right after the ordination. Furthermore, 42% of these former priests either fell in love or desired for an intimate relationship or marriage.

Fernandez (2001) also found that priests described marriage as the only alternative path to priesthood. However, Brent (1991) argued that marriage may be one of the options for some priests who have thought of leaving the priesthood. He added that, marriage is a transitional phase in its own way. Moreover, Schoenherr and Greeley (1974) revealed that the desire for an intimate relationship or marriage is the most essential factor within favor of staying or leaving the priesthood.

Struggle with Celibacy

Celibacy is a matter of discipline and is not essential to the priesthood (Leaving the Priesthood, n.d); it is an abstinence from any sort of sexual intercourse (VandenBos, 2006). One of the reasons of priests in leaving the priesthood is to argue with the mandatory celibacy that the Catholic Church demands from them. Struggle with celibacy is another common reason among the priests to leave the priesthood (Guillen, 2009; Sunardi, 2014). Hoge (as cited in Guillen, 2009) found that struggle with celibacy is the second most common reason of priestly departure after the desire for an intimate relationship or marriage.

Similarly, in a survey of Fichter (2009) among 131 former Catholic priests, 105 (80.2%) became Episcopalian priests, 15 (11.5%) Lutheran priests, eight (6.1) Congregationalist priests, and three (2.3%) Methodist priests. When Fichter (2009) asked the former Catholic priests why they left the Roman Catholic Church, 6 out of 10 former Catholic priests reported about the struggle of celibacy. In addition, Hoge (as cited in Guillen, 2009) found that 20% to 30% of priests left the priesthood because most of them argued with mandatory celibacy of the Roman Catholic Church.

Schoenherr and Greeley (1974) also found that the struggle with celibacy is another factor in making decision to leave the priesthood. However, they argued that the celibacy issue is by no means having sexual desire or desire for an intimate relationship or marriage. They added that, celibacy refers to moving into unorthodox social relationships with a woman. Thus, it focuses more with the celibacy requirements of the Roman Catholic Church and other church denominations (Schoenherr & Greeley, 1974). However, Hickson and Gudz (1995) argued that the ethical or moral differences with church positions should be considered to explain the phenomenon of priestly departure, though the struggle with celibacy and the desire for an intimate relationship and marriage which were reasons given by those priests who left the priesthood. On the other hand, many studies showed that priesthood is a lifelong calling and is therefore, permanent (e.g Pietkiewicz, 2016; Isacco, et al. 2014). Thus, it not appropriate to say 'ex-priest' or even 'ex-clergy' (Fernandez, 2001).

Conflict/Disagreement with Church Authority

Celibacy is not the only reason why priests leave the priesthood (Leaving the Priesthood, n.d). Greeley (2004) showed that conflict or disagreement with church authorities is another factor of priestly departure and is considered a major source of neuroses (VandenBos, 2006). According to Greeley (2004), this serves as the second common reason why priest would decide to leave the priesthood. In the study of Kane (2008) about the perception and attitudes of priests toward Bishops, the result showed that most of them felt disrespect for their Bishops as well as a sense of betrayal from church authorities.

Similarly, in the study of Hoge and Okure (2006) among international priests, they found that the majority of them had conflict and disagreement with church authorities specifically with their Bishops. According to Hoge (as cited in Guillen, 2009) between 30% and 40% of priests left the priesthood because most of them were disillusioned with their fellow priests and had subordinate-superior relationship problems (Fernandez, 2001). Hoge (as cited in Guillen, 2009) reported that conflict or disagreement with church authorities is considered as the third common reason for priestly departure after the desire for an intimate relationship or marriage and struggle with celibacy. Moreover, the lack of social support from the church authorities may lead to priestly departure as well. Sunardi (2014) stated that social support has positive effects against the vocational crisis of the priestly life.

According to Fernandez (2001), some diocesan priests complained issues of unfair treatment and favoritism among the clergy. In addition, some priests were treated by their Bishop or Superior as children rather than adults (Blomjous, as cited in Hickson & Gudz, 1995). This is in contrary to what the priests promised during their ordination wherein, whatever required assignments were given by the Bishop, they would readily accept it. However, since some assignments were not desirable for some priests, it would lead to conflict or disagreement with the church authorities (Leaving the Priesthood, n.d).

Schallert and Kelly (1970) studied the 'crucial other' in times of vocational crisis of the priestly life; they found that this crucial other is not necessarily a woman that influences a priest's choice to leave the priesthood. Rather, it could be a fellow priest, Bishop, religious Superior, or Spiritual Director whom a priest trusts and admires. However, this may also result to a vocational change or priestly departure if a priest did not receive social support from church authorities (Guillen, 2009; Sunardi, 2014).

Brent (1991) considered the church authorities as one of the reasons of priestly departure. DellaCava (1975) also found that the expressions of dissatisfaction in priestly life and relationships with fellow priests and the Bishop are evident for priestly commitment to the priesthood. However, this may also result to role conflict of a priest if lack of social support happens. Their challenges and difficulties, therefore, include problems with their fellow priests, Bishop, and church leaders (Cornelio, 2012). Moreover, the most common complaint of the priests was the way authority is exercised in the church (New York Times, as cited in DellaCava 1975).

Lack of Personal Skills to meet Pastoral Demands

Lack of personal skills to meet pastoral demands or struggling with personal and psychological problems is another reason of priestly departure (Potvin & Muncada, as cited in Sunardi, 2014). Some priests had suffered from alcoholism or drinking problems which roots from work-related stresses and leads to lack of personal skills to meet the pastoral and church demands (Sunardi, 2014).

In the study of Kennedy, Heckler, Kobler, and Walker (1977), they conducted a clinical assessment of the priesthood and interviewed 218 American priests. The results showed that 57% of the priests seemed to be underdeveloped and eight percent were maldeveloped. Kennedy et al. (1977) reported that their lives as a priest were shaped by the expectations of society, having comrades or acquaintances, but no close friends, exhibiting a lack of understanding of their own lives, and handling their emotions through defense mechanisms such as rationalization and repression. Moreover, while they may be successful in their ministry, they may be unfulfilled personally. Similarly, according to a study commissioned by the U.S Bishops, 40% of American priests reported "having severe personal, behavioral or mental problems in the previous 12 months" (Rice, as cited in Hickson & Gudz, 1995, p. 23) right after the ordination to priesthood.

Hoge and Wenger (as cited in Louque, 2006) found that loss of confidence among priests exists and may also result to priestly departure. In the study of Schoenherr and Young (1990) among 36,370 resigned and active priests from 1966 to 1984, 50% to 60% of priests left the priesthood in 1968 through 1974, while 32% to 44% of priests left in 1975 through 1984. Similarly, Hoge (as cited in Guillen, 2009) studied that between 5% and 10% left the priesthood because they did not find themselves in the ministry. Moreover, 95% of priests who have strong religious values left after four years in the priesthood and 81% of priests left after 6 to 8 years of being a priest (Rulla, Riddick, & Imoda, 1976).

Kelly (as cited in Fernandez, 2001) found that satisfaction of one's role in the ministry is found to be related to priestly commitment and priestly departure. Many studies (e.g Guillen, 2009; Rulla, Riddick, & Imoda, 1976) showed that those priests who left the priesthood had a lack of collegiality, incapacitated to make personal choices in life, and lack of personal skills to meet pastoral demands (Leaving the Priesthood, n.d).

Sexual Orientation Issue

The Church Doctrine is involved in forming the self-image of a priest (Brent, 1991). Consequently, one of the frustrations of a priest today is his search for self-identity (Rausch, as cited in Hickson & Gudz, 1995). VandenBos (2006) defined homosexuality and bisexuality as a same-sex sexual orientation or activity. Many priests leave the priesthood over the issue of homosexuality and bisexuality since a high percentage of priests and Bishops are considered as homosexual and bisexual in the Roman Catholic Church (Leaving the Priesthood, n.d). In the study of Hoge (as cited in Guillen, 2009), between 5% and 15% of priests leave the priesthood because of a relationship with another man as well as the desire for a long-term relationship. He added that, the number of gay priests in the Roman Catholic Church could be as high as 50%. Similarly, Toufexis (as cited in Fernandez, 2001) found that 10% to 13% of priests had intimacies with adult men while six percent had a relationship with adolescents.

Age Factor

VandenBos (2006) has associated age factor with the inner conflicts coming at a particular stage of a priestly life. According to Schoenherr and Young (1990), the critical period of leaving the priesthood usually begins five years after ordination; they found that priests leave the priesthood between the ages 30 and 40 during 1970 to 1974. However, the age bracket changed to 35 to 39 during 1980 to 1984. Similarly, Hoge (as cited in Guillen, 2009) found that the priests usually leave the priesthood between ages 35 and 39. Moreover, priests who have the thought of leaving the priesthood are more likely to be younger, hold big responsibilities, and have experienced burn-out in the ministry (e.g Fernandez, 2001; Rossetti, 2011; Schoenherr & Greeley, 1974). However, according to Sunardi (2014), age factor "may suggest not only the atmosphere in which priests and seminarians live, but also the struggle within the church" (p. 14).

Some studies found that those priests who left the priesthood were ordained at an earlier age than those who remained in the ministry (e.g. Guillen, 2009; Rossetti, 2011; Sunardi; 2014; Verdieck, Shields, & Hoge, 1988). Hoge (as cited in Guillen, 2009) noted that priestly departure had increased from 3% to 9% in 1990 and in 2002, it increased to 12 %. He added that, the mechanism of age factor could affect both the priestly commitment and priestly departure. Similarly, an article entitled Fact Sheet on Crisis Caused by Priest Shortage (as cited in Hickson & Gudz, 1995) indicated that almost 42% of all American priests leave the priesthood within 25 years and half of all American priests were under the age of 60. In addition, VandenBos (2006) described that age and stages of the priestly life refer to priests' psychological maturity.

Results

Conflict with the Bishop is one distinct theme that emerged in my interview with one of the former priests. According to him, this conflict stemmed not from being able to understand each other's perspectives (*we had differences*). Another distinct theme that surfaced from my interview with the former priests is the struggle with celibacy (*the quality of celibacy becomes meaningless*), wherein, according to him, this is what the priesthood demanded of him and required by the Bishop. Disappointment/Discouragement with fellow priests (*some priests who would gamble*), and lack of spiritual/human formation (*we did not have much spiritual practices*) are also distinct themes that emerged from my interview among the former priests. One of the former priests admitted that he was disappointed by his fellow priests who would gamble up to early hours in the morning. Also, the other one had experienced lack of spiritual practices in the ministry. The former priests unveiled that:

"*I… and my Bishop did not see each other eye to eye… we had differences.*" (Fr. Matthew)

"So, basically, if you're not faithful with obedience, nawawara din itong quality kan celibacy."

(So, basically, if you're not faithful with obedience, the quality of celibacy also becomes

meaningless in a sense). (Fr. Luke)

"...we could not go on with relative priest would mind us, our activities in the parish or would

make us feel that we were not part of the parish... That's why, I, myself, experienced the way

associate priest being treated." (Fr. Matthew)

"Another thing, during our time, my time, we did not have much spiritual practices like the

annual retreat." (Fr. Matthew)

Encountering problems when it comes to the system of the church may also result to the

internal factors affecting the priestly commitment of the former priests. Moreover, feeling of

loneliness (*I was no longer happy*) is one distinct theme that emerged from my interview among

the former priests. According to him, he found that he was not happy anymore with the priestly

life. Also, lack of interest with the priestly life (*I was not engrossed or interested*) was admitted

by one of the former priests because he was not interested with what the priest does in the

priesthood and he had other interests. By then, realizing that priesthood is not fit for the person

(*this is not for me*), are common reasons among the former priests. Aside from these reasons,

unfulfilled career desire of a former priest (*I was not given a celebret*) also emerged as a distinct

theme when he did not fulfill his career desire aside from being a priest. The former priests

affirmed that:

"...someday, when I finally decided to leave because I was no longer happy... When I found out

that I was no longer happy... That's why my life was no longer happy." (Fr. Mark)

"...I was not so interested with the work of a priest." (Fr. Mark)

"Dae ko 'to naisip hanggang sa… hanggang sa pagka-padi ko, saka ko lang na-realized na… this is not for me… bako talaga ini ang buhay ko." (I never thought about it before (leaving the priesthood) until… when I became a priest, I just realized that… this is not for me… this is not really my life.) (Fr. Luke)

"… I intended to study in Manila to take up an… engineering, I was not given a celebret…I did receive a celebret but it was only given for one week and so I had to come back." (Fr. Matthew)

More so, external factors such as having a relationship with a woman (*I had a relationship with women*) and having a child or family (*I opted to be a responsible man*) also emerged as factors affecting the priestly commitment. The former priests added that:

"…kasi kan nasa seminary pa lang ako, I was having a relationship with women."

(...because when I was still inside the seminary, I was having a relationship with women).

(Fr. Luke)

"I opted to be a responsible family man than creating scandal at the expense of priesthood."

(Fr. John)

The aforementioned themes imply not only the factors affecting priestly commitment but also resulting to some serious psychological consequences such as 'social-stigma'. Overall, four themes were common among the former priests and six were distinct as shown in Table 1.

Table 1. *Common and distinct themes for underlying factors of priestly departure*

Former Priests	Common Themes	Distinct Themes
Fr. Matthew	Lack of spiritual/human formation; Having a relationship with a woman	Conflict with Bishop; Disappointment/Discouragement with fellow priests,
Fr. Luke	Realizing that priesthood is not fit for the person	Unfulfilled career desire; Struggling with celibacy
Fr. Mark	Having a child or family	
Fr. John		Feeling of loneliness; Lack of interest with the priestly life

A priest's departure could be considered by the factors that originated from the system of the church. *Conflict with the Bishop* is one of the factors found to be the reason why former priest left the priesthood. This implies that their Superiors, specifically their Bishop, made him feel that he was not being supported. Aside from that, a priest's personal decision is incongruent with the decision of his Bishop. The perception of man support received from the Bishop may have prompted the priest to leave the priesthood. This finding could be understood in the context of what Adler (as cited in McLeod, 2007) believed that when a person becomes overwhelmed and prevented to accomplish a goal, this feeling of being inferior serves as a hindrance for positive accomplishment and would result to abandoning priestly vocation.

Aside from the promises of a priest with obedience and poverty to his Bishop during the ordination to the priesthood, he also needs to abstain himself from any sexual intercourse. However, *struggling with celibacy* emerged as a factor affecting the priestly commitment. Priest who struggles with celibacy may decide to abandon his priestly vocation when he feels that he is not faithful with his promise to follow the virtue of celibacy that the Catholic Church demands.

Moreover, *Disappointment or discouragement with fellow priests* contributes to priestly departure. When a priest's relationship with his fellow priests becomes disillusioned, a priest, therefore, may decide to leave the priesthood. This implies that the harmonious relationship of a priest with his fellow priests could determine his motivation to continue the priesthood or not. However, if a priest feels disillusionment with his fellow priests, he may no longer have a reason to stay with the priesthood.

Similarly, *Lack of Spiritual and Human Formation* also found as another factor. Ever since, a priest is being formed about spiritual and human formations in his entire life of being a seminarian. However, when a priest finally got ordained, usually the formation also ends. This implies that having a conflict with the Bishop and feeling of disappointment or discouragement with fellow priests could be understood because of the lack of spiritual and human formation in the priesthood.

A priest's departure is considered as personal when these factors affecting his priestly vocation do not come from the system of the church but coming from within. *Feeling of loneliness* is one of the factors that affect priestly commitment to the priesthood. This feeling of loneliness could lead to some factors which affect his priestly commitment such as *lack of interest with the priestly life, realizing that priesthood is not fit for the person*, and *having unfulfilled career desire in the priestly life*. This finding could be understood through Rogers (as cited in McLeod, 2014) that, in order for a priest to be a fully functioning person, his ideal-self and real-self must be congruent. Therefore, if his real-self and his ideal-self are incongruent with the priestly life, this would just lead to a not fully functioning person. As a result, he would just leave the priesthood.

Finally, a priest could leave the priesthood because of external factors which affect his priestly commitment. *Having a relationship with a woman* is one of the factors, wherein, a priest endows the Filipino concept of 'family'. Hence, *having a child or family* is considered as a view of commitment to not seeing the self as a fully individuated creature, but rather, a person who is in need of love and to be loved. This finding could be aligned with Maslow's Theory (as cited in McLeod, 2016), wherein, one of the physiological needs of a person is the need for having a child or family. Therefore, a priest's departure is not just the woman herself, but rather the family itself which is seen to be his moral obligation.

CHAPTER FOUR

Psychological Consequences of Leaving the Priesthood

Weber and Wheaton (as cited in Hickson & Gudz, 1995) interviewed 88 former priests about their experiences after leaving the priesthood. They found that most of the former priests had experienced a number of injustices such as being labeled as a public sinner, an enemy, an embarrassment, being called as 'Judas', receiving little amount of money, and being blocked in employment opportunities. In addition, former priests were forbidden to wear clerical dress, discouraged to administer Sacraments, and reduced to guilt ridden, isolated, confused, and anxious being a displaced person (Catholic Answers Staff, 2016).

Similarly, Rakosza (2016) found that those priests who left the priesthood have no alternatives afterwards. Leaving the priesthood is not acceptable in the society and former priests would find it difficult to build a new relationship with others as they enter their new career. Moreover, civil life for former priests seems to be frustrated. On the other hand, former priests have received little or no support from others about their decision in leaving the priesthood (Schoenherr & Young, 1993). Consequently, former priests were expected to live as super human beings since society expects highly of them (Hickson & Gudz, 1995). Fichter (2009) also found that former priests were described as lax Christians, bad, foolish, and immature with their decision in leaving the priesthood. In addition, Pietkiewicz (2016) studied that former priests have experienced shame, guilt, stigma-related fear, becoming an object of scandal in the church, receiving negative response from other priests and lay people, and concerned about losing social support. However, Yalom (1985) argued that despite the decision of the former priests in leaving the priesthood, they would still be welcomed in the society.

Results

Four themes described the psychological consequences of leaving the priesthood emerged during my interview with the former priests. *Difficulty in looking for work/resources* (*it was so hard to look for work*) is one of the immediate challenges that these former priests have faced; obviously, going back to their ordinary life outside the ministry called for a stable source of income. Then, the decision of the former priests in leaving the priesthood had brought some emotional consequences such as experiencing social-stigma (*You will become a social-stigma*) which is a common theme for the former priests. According to him, people looked at him differently and had experienced a number of injustices in the society. Moreover, difficulty in adjusting to the secular life (*I found it hard*) also emerged as a common theme, whereas, difficulty in living independently (*independent out of my parents*) also found to be related among the former priests. The former priests revealed that:

"... pag yaon ka sa laog kan pagkapadi, mataas ang paghiling sa pagkapadi, kung ga'no kataas ang paghiling saimo kadto, iyo man an pagbilis kan pagbagsak mo." (...when you're in the priesthood, priests are perceived as superior, consequently, it would be an opposite of it if one has decided to leave the priesthood) (Fr. Luke)

"...when I finally decided to live the daily life of a lay man, it was really hard for me to adjust to the world." (Fr. Mark)

"My experience when I was in Manila...it was so hard to look for work or a job." (Fr. Mark)

"My problem then was... how I would live outside... independent out of my parents."

(Fr. John)

In leaving the priesthood, former priests struggled from both internal and external consequences to adjust to the secular life. Their adjustments include coping mechanisms such as accepting the consequences of their departure. Overall, three themes were common among the former priests and one theme was distinct as shown in Table 2.

Table 2. *Common and distinct themes for psychological consequences after leaving the priesthood*

Former Priests	Common Themes	Distinct Themes
Fr. Matthew Fr. Luke Fr. Mark Fr. John	Difficulty in looking for work/resources; Experiencing social-sigma; Difficulty in adjusting to the secular life	Difficulty in living independently

For some priests, leaving the priesthood is one of the hardest decisions to do because of a number of injustices in the society. Consequently, when he finally decides to abandon his priestly vocation, one of the psychological consequences that he has to face is social-stigma. *Experiencing social-stigma* is considered as one of the consequences of leaving knowing that leaving the priesthood is not acceptable and considered as taboo in the society. With this, when a former priest experiences social-stigma, it would be difficult for him to adjust to the secular life. Then, stigmatizing continues even with the work that a former priest found. Moreover, *difficulty in adjusting to the secular life* is also a psychological consequence, wherein, from experiencing social-stigma, a priest returns to the life of an ordinary lay person. However, people would look at him differently and would experience isolation from community.

Aside from experiencing social-stigma and finding difficulty in adjusting to the secular life, difficulty in looking for work or resources also emerged as a consequence of a priest's departure. *Difficulty in looking for work or resources* is seemed to be maladjusted for some priests who left the priesthood. Similarly, when a former priest finds it hard to look for a job, it is also difficult for him to live independently from his family. *Difficulty in living independently* is another psychological consequence in which a former priest needs to provide his daily sustenance as well as his basic needs on his own without the support from his family.

CHAPTER FIVE

Adjustments to the Secular Life

Pietkiewicz (2016) stated that individuals who decided to change their vocation are encouraged to take counseling to help their situations. According to Hickson and Gudz (1995), the personal relationships of the former priests with others are usually distant, highly stylized, unrewarding, have limited opportunities to explore their interpersonal growth, closed to the feedback of a single viewpoint, have difficulties in transitional phase, have underdeveloped psychosocial identities, have difficulty and discomfort in a specific place, and identify themselves with the role of the priesthood instead of their own identities. However, Arackal (2015) argued that former priests could live a normal life; society does not impose any limitations as long as they attend services in the church, confess, and receives the Holy Communion. Furthermore, Betz (2004) noted that Psychologist could help former priests cope with their decision in leaving the priesthood, plan for new qualifications, and job-hunting for their career development.

After experiencing a lot of psychological consequences, former priests were on the process of adjustment to the secular life such as: rationalizing about the decision in leaving (*But for me, all professions are vocation*), identifying own experiences with others (*If they (priests) were not able to marry their partners*), accepting the consequences/risks (*I took the risks*), and receiving support from others (*I have a Ninang (godmother) who helped me then*). The former priests emphasized that:

"...But for me, all professions are vocation... all professions are calling... different kinds of calling... calling to be a teacher, calling to be a priest, calling to be an engineer, nurse, etc. So, they are all vocations." (Fr. Mark)

"If they (priests) were not able to marry their partners, so may mga alanganin… there were hesitations about it." (If they (priests) were not able to marry their partners, so there were hesitations… there were hesitations about it) (Fr. Mark)

"So, paano mo masi-save an sadiri mo dyan? So, I took the risks… I faced the risks with acceptance." (So, how would you save yourself from that situation? So, I took the risks… I faced the risks with acceptance) (Fr. Luke)

"Luckily, my aunt, who was working with _______ (government agency) helped me up." (Fr. Matthew)

For former priests, when they finally adjusted to the life of a lay man, it is therefore a need for them to view their future life as a lay person such as being employed. Overall, three themes were common among the former priests, and one theme was distinct as shown in Table 3.

Table 3. *Common and distinct themes for adjustment to the secular life*

Former Priests	Common Themes	Distinct Themes
Fr. Matthew	Identifying own experiences with others;	Receiving support from others
Fr. Luke		
Fr. Mark	Rationalizing about the decision in leaving;	
Fr. John	Accepting the consequences/risks	

After experiencing a lot of psychological consequences in leaving the priesthood, a former priest is on the process of adjustment to the secular life, wherein, he has to live the daily life of a lay man through rationalization and identification. *Rationalizing about the decision in leaving* is considered as one of the adjustments of a former priest to the secular life. This implies that a former priest thinks that everything happens for a reason and God has a purpose for him. Similarly, *identifying own experiences with others* is another adjustment when a priest leaves the priesthood, wherein, a former priest identifies his own experiences with those priests who also left the priesthood and had the same experiences like him. For a former priest, he is not the only one who experiences a number of injustices in the society, but others also experience these.

A former priest who decided to leave the priesthood accepts the consequences and takes the risks as he returns to the life of a lay man and receives support from others. For a former priest, *accepting the consequences or risks* is one of the best things to do in order for him to adjust himself to the secular life. Despite his decision in leaving the priesthood, *receiving support from others* is also a way of his adjustment without receiving any judgment from other people. Through acceptance and support, it would be easy for a former priest to accept the fact that he could still live a normal life and society itself cannot impose any limitations to him.

When a former priest is finally adjusted to the life of a lay man, *being employed for a job* is the first thing to do for his future life as a lay person. Fortunately, he is able to be employed for a job and accept work opportunities. Despite his decision in leaving the priesthood, still, there are works being offered to him. Also, being employed for a job is said to be his fulfilment and at the same time, a new life for him after leaving the priesthood and finally adjusted to the secular life.

CHAPTER SIX

Views of Future Life as a Lay Person

DellaCava (1975) interviewed 35 former priests regarding their future life as lay people. He found that 18 have been involved in parish work, six are full time students, and 11 served as teachers or are in specialized positions. Among the former priests, 24 of them served as an active priest for more than five years while 11 served less than five years in the ministry. In addition, among all of them, seven still have plans to get married in the Roman Catholic Church.

Many of the former priests who left the priesthood are still connected with the Roman Catholic Church and asked for a laicization or dispensation from the Vatican to get married within the church (Leaving the Priesthood, n.d). In fact, according to a survey of one Bishop, 78% of the former priests continued their membership within the Roman Catholic Church (Fichter, 2009). Moreover, Arackal (2015) stated that most of the former priests still live like a priest, active in social works and prayers, and others got married.

However, most of the former priests claimed that it was not worth leaving the priesthood (Arackal, 2015). Some are still concerned about the confidentiality of their departure and want to maintain their positive image in the society (Isacco et al., 2014). Despite the fact that many priests have already left the priesthood, the Roman Catholic Church still believes that "once a priest, always a priest" (Hebrews 7:17).

After turning back from vocation they once vowed, the former priests viewed their future life as being employed for a job (*Then, I was encouraged to _________ (name of a company)*). According to one of the former priests, he looked for a job right after leaving the priesthood. To be dispensed/laicized (*I got through the dispensation*) and being married to the church (*I'm a married person*) are also common themes among the former priests who viewed their lives to be dispensed and married to the Catholic Church.

Continuing their membership in the church (*I was called to under a parish work*) was also found as a common theme among the former priests despite their decision in leaving the priesthood. One of the former priests admitted that he is satisfied in his present life (*That's why I'm enjoying my life now*) and emerged as a distinct theme among the former priests. According to him, despite the decision he made, still, there are no regrets because his life had a direction and focus on what he does in his present life. The former priests stated that:

"…Then, I was encouraged to __________ (name of a company) and I became a publishing mentor, so I give programs about financial literacy, financial counselling, sa klase nin finances. So, magayon and teacher na ako sa ginigibo ko ngunyan, to empower." (…Then, I was encouraged to _______ (name of a company) and I became a publishing mentor, so I give programs about financial literacy, financial counselling, different kinds of finances. So, it's nice and I am a teacher for what I am doing right now, to empower) (Fr. Luke)

"I got through with the dispensation… after so many years!" (Fr. Mark)

"…well, married na kaya ako ngunyan…I just had my dispensation kumbaga approved na kan Roma na ako pwede na akong mag-agom." (Well, I'm married now, I'm married. I just had my dispensation with approval from Rome allowing me to marry) (Fr. Luke)

"Sa mga Padi, ini-invite ako sa saindang mga prayer meetings… I give talks to their Parishioners." (For some priests, they are inviting me for their prayer meetings... I give talks to their Parishioners) (Fr. Luke)

"…Tapos, the good thing ngunyan na dispensed na ako, maogma ako sa ginigibo ko. That's why I'm enjoying my life now… Kumbaga, focus." (…Then, the good thing now that I am

dispensed already, I am happy with what I am doing. That's why I'm enjoying my life now... In other words, focus) (Fr. Luke)

The aforementioned reasons, psychological consequences, adjustments, and views of future life as a lay person of the former priests have brought a sudden understanding about the phenomenon of priestly departure in the Philippine context. Overall, four themes were common among the former priests and one theme was distinct as shown in Table 4.

Table 4. *Common and distinct themes for views of future life as a lay person*

Former Priests	Common Themes	Distinct Themes
Fr. Matthew Fr. Luke Fr. Mark Fr. John	Being employed for a job; Being dispensed/laicized; Being married in the church; Continuing membership in the church	Being satisfied in a present life

When a priest leaves the priesthood, one of the options is to apply for a dispensation or laicization in order to marry within the Catholic Church. *Being dispensed or laicized* is another view of future life as a lay person of a priest who left the priesthood. Applying for dispensation would help a former priest to adjust to the secular life because he is still concerned about the confidentiality of his departure and wants to maintain his positive image in the society despite his decision in leaving the priesthood. Hence, *being married in the church* is a result once a former priest finally received his dispensation from Vatican.

Finally, when a former priest is totally adjusted to the secular life, the view of the self begins to come out. *Continuing membership in the church* is said to be considered as one of the former priest's views of his future life after leaving the priesthood. Moreover, despite the challenges and difficulties that a former priest experiences such as shame and social-stigma, still, he is satisfied with his decision in leaving the priesthood. Former priest's life out of the priesthood has a direction and *being satisfied in a present life* is the affirmation of the self; wherein, a former priest has no regrets. It implies that he is now happy of what he does and most importantly, he finds a true meaning to his life that is significant to him at present. At the end of the day, no one might help him to move forward; but he – alone with the mercy and grace of Omnipotent and Omniscient God.

CHAPTER SEVEN

Implications

Theoretical Implications. The main theoretical contributions of this study include the new findings about the psychological consequences of leaving the priesthood, adjustments to the secular life, and views of future life as a lay person. Most of the previous studies have focused only to various reasons of priestly departure. In this study, three unique underlying factors of leaving the priesthood were identified: lack of spiritual/human formation, unfulfilled career desire, and having a child or family.

This study also contributes to previous study on priestly departure in the Philippines (Fernandez, 2001). Similarly, this study found that woman is by no means the reason why a priest leaves the priesthood. However, the study of Fernandez (2001) did not determine the psychological consequences, adjustments, and views of future life of diocesan priests who left the priesthood. Results of this study also showed that there are distinctions between the foreign priest departure from Filipino priest's departure such as the familial concept which is seen to be as a 'moral obligation'.

Finally, this study attempted to emphasize the priestly departure in the Philippine context knowing that there are only few studies who attempted to demystify the phenomenon of priestly departure in the Philippines. Moreover, previous studies did not explore the present life of diocesan priests who left the priesthood. In this study, it is found that the priests who left are still connected within the Catholic Church despite their decision in leaving the priesthood. Furthermore, this study also depicts the popular belief of some people that priest leaves the priesthood because of a woman only.

Practical Implications. The experiences of priests who left priesthood gave them a voice to defend themselves from criticisms regarding their decision in leaving. This study, therefore, serves as an avenue to hear their sides and know the factors that affect priestly commitment. Moreover, this study emphasized that priests who left the priesthood are in need of counselling and therapy in order for them to adjust in the secular life and move forward after leaving the priesthood.

Since most of the studies have focused on the various reasons of priestly departure, the other factors such as psychological consequences, adjustments, and views of future life as a lay person did not explore psychologically. In this study, it is clear that priestly departure entails psychological consequences. Priests who left are still on the process of reviving themselves as well as helping them in a transitional phase of their life.

Furthermore, this study suggests a formation program for those priests who left the priesthood, helping their situations in the society. It also highlights the priestly formation that is needed to be observed by the priests so that there would be less asking for dispensation or laicization. Practically, it is a call for the Catholic Church to be open with this phenomenon of priestly departure.

CHAPTER EIGHT

Recommendations

Catholic Church through the Bishops

The Bishops may offer on going formation programs to cater the psychological and spiritual needs of priests. Also, it is a need for constant dialogue with priests to listen to their problems and difficulties in the priesthood. Moreover, the diocese may help the former priests adjust to the secular life despite their decision in leaving the priesthood. The Catholic Church should still be considered as a 'home' of the former priests.

Priestly Formation

The formation should not end during the ordination to the priesthood of a priest. Bishops, priests, and seminarians should be aware of the formation they undergo. Priestly formation should be a long-lasting formation not just in the seminary.

Future Researchers

Another further study should be conducted which includes former priests who belong to other religious congregations. Also, further research on why priests would decide to go to other place specifically abroad after leaving the priesthood.

Recommendations from Former Diocesan Priests

"Well, what I would like to recommend as what I have stated in my petition for regular session, seminarians should be informed about other denominations… about other churches so that they are given the whole picture of what priestly is…" -Father Matthew

---

"Balance… Balance sa formation…dapat balance ang mind and heart. Kung ang formation nagpo-focus lang sa mind, then, nakukulangan ang heart, sa human formation, garo 'yan hydrocephalus. Dakulaon ang brain, saditon ang heart. So, balance ang duwang iyan… Tapos, ang spiritual formation pagnaka-padi na… s'yempre so formation kan mga padi. So, ayan… balance." (Balance... Balance in formation... mind and heart should be balanced. If the focus of the formation is only the mind, and lacking in heart, in human formation, it seems like a hydrocephalus. The mind is so big, whereas, the heart is so small. So, both of them need to be balanced… Then, the spiritual formation when one got finally ordained, of course, the formation of the priests should still be observable… So, balance.) -Father Luke

---

"Seminary life should be adjusted to the life of the world. The seminary training should not be… or the seminary training should be adjusted to the world. It does not mean that if you're adjusting to the life of the world, you will be seeking for the opposite sex… na para bang dae ka mabibigla to adjust to the world. That's why when you finish the priesthood, there are no more so many adjustments…" (Seminary life should be adjusted to the life of the world. The seminary training should not be… or the seminary training should be adjusted to the world. It does not mean that if you're adjusting to the life of the world, you will be seeking for the opposite-sex… in order for

you not to be surprised to adjust to the world. That's why when you finish priesthood, adjustments will be lesser…) -Father Mark

---

"…There was homesickness especially after long vacation particularly Christmas vacations, adjustment to living in a large community, adjustment to studies…misunderstanding with teachers and formators and more… although new found freedom away from seminary structures, the allure of the worldly cultures start creeping in to my priestly life affecting my prayer life most."

-Father John

CHAPTER NINE

Methods and Procedures

In the Philippine context, there were only few studies about the phenomenon of priestly departure (e.g Fernandez, 2001). Moreover, there were limited studies who conducted sexual orientation, age factor, psychological consequences of leaving the priesthood, adjustments to the secular life, and views of future life as a lay person of the former priests regarding their decision in leaving the priesthood.

Previous studies about priestly departure used large-scales surveys to gather data from the respondents (e.g. Cornelio, 2012; DellaCava, 1975; Pietkiewicz, 2016; Sunardi, 2014). A number of studies have focused on various reasons or factors affecting the decision of a priest to leave the priesthood (Fernandez, 2001; Greeley, 2004; Guillen, 2009), psychological consequences of leaving the priesthood (Hickson & Gudz, 1995; Rakosza, 2016), adjustment to the secular life (Arackal, 2015; Pope, 2015) and view of future life as lay people (DellaCava, 1975; Pietkiewicz, 2016). Also, most of the previous studies have focused on former and foreign religious priests who left the priesthood. Few studies used qualitative research design, specifically descriptive case study method (e.g Fernandez, 2001), to determine the factors affecting priestly commitment.

This study used qualitative research design, specifically descriptive case study method, to determine the underlying factors of leaving the priesthood. Face-to-face interview was used to gather data in the study. Face-to-face interview is a useful way of conducting a research that aims to describe reality and to establish prevalence of a specific phenomenon (Mathers, Fox, & Hunn, 2007). In addition, this approach is commonly used to gather information about attitudes and behaviors of a certain group of people that aims to show what is happening in a certain phenomenon at a particular time.

In this study, data was collected through a face-to-face interview using a semi-structured interview schedule composed of 12-item open-ended questions. Face-to-face interview is used to achieve high quality data from a subject matter that is sensitive (Mathers, Fox, & Hunn, 2007). Face-to-face interview allows the researcher to establish rapport with participants and gain their cooperation. It also allows the researcher to ask follow-up questions, gather more and deeper information (Leedy & Ormrod, 2001).

To determine the underlying factors why former diocesan priests left the priesthood, four former diocesan priests from two different dioceses in the Bicol region were located. They were chosen through snowball and convenient sampling techniques. The participants' age ranged from 43 to 70 and has at least served the priesthood for 1 to 12 years. I sent them letters of invitation attached to the letters were the consent forms, delivered personally and through Facebook chat. I asked them if they could participate in the study. The face-to-face interview was conducted separately for each participant at their respective homes and offices.

For ethical considerations, I asked permission from the participants if the interview could be recorded through a voice recorder. I also informed them that I would be taking note of our conversation. I changed the name of the persons, schools, and organizations mentioned during the interview to protect their identities and privacy. Moreover, the participants were informed about the confidentiality of the data.

Before the data analysis, I sent copies of the interview transcript to the participants to check the accuracy of the recording. Then, I asked two-raters to validate the themes that I have identified. To identify the themes within the data, I followed Braun and Clarke's (2006) six phases of Thematic Analysis. First, I familiarized myself with the data by reading the transcript several times. During this phase, I cited down key ideas that emerged. Then, I systematically coded each statement of the participants. After coding, I clustered all the responses according to their common themes.

The samples of the study were limited to former diocesan priests only. Former religious priests were not included in the study. It could have been better if the samples considered are larger and included other former priests from other congregations.

CHAPTER TEN

Reflexivity

In the Philippines, priestly departure is considered as 'taboo' in the society. When a seminarian or a priest decides to leave the priesthood, people usually think that the primary reason for leaving is a woman. As a former seminarian, I came up with the decision to study the phenomenon of priestly departure in the Philippine context. Literally, one of the books that made me inspire to further investigate about leaving the priesthood was the book written by Fr. Fernandez – a priest residing in the Philippines.

Moreover, I have heard a lot of news about priestly departure in the Philippines such as a priest who ran in politics, got married, had sexual abuse issue, and so forth. Consequently, a priest who left the priesthood has no voice to defend himself from criticisms and judgments; it is also a stigma in the society that a former priest has no right to speak and raise his freedom as a human being. Furthermore, I want to serve as a voice on their behalf; I attempt to correct the popular belief of some people that a seminarian or a priest leaves the priesthood because of a woman only. This issue is a need to be addressed not only in the Catholic Church, but also of the people who seem to consider this phenomenon a mortal sin. The question is, 'Who is really infallible?'

> *"You are a priest forever; a priest like Melchizedek of old."*
> -Hebrews 7:17-

Amen.

REFERENCES

Arackal, C., M. (2015). Priests: what it is like to leave the priesthood? Retrieved October 16, 2016 from https://www.quora.com/Priests-What-is-it-like-to-leave-the-priesthood

Betz, N. E. (2004). Contributions of self-efficacy theory to career counseling: A personal perspective. *Career Development Quarterly, 52*(4), 340-353.

Braun, V., & Clarke, V. (2006). Using thematic analysis in psychology. *Qualitative Research In Psychology, 3*(2), 77-101.

Brent, J.S. (1991). Existential group therapy as a treatment modality for exiting Christian fundamentalists. *Counseling and Values, 35*, 228-231.

Catholic Answers Staff. (2016). Does laicization remove a priest's powers? Retrieved October 15, 2016 from http://www.catholic.com/quickquestions/does-laicization remove-a-priests-powers

Catholic Answers Staff. (2016). When a priest leaves. Retrieved October 15, 2016 from http://catholicstraightanswers.com/if-a-priest-leaves-the-priesthood-is-he-still-able-to-perform-the-sacraments/

Cornelio, J., S. (2012). Priesthood satisfaction and the challenges priests face: A case study of a rural diocese in the Philippines. *Religions. 3*, 1103-119.

DellaCava, F. A. (1975). Becoming an ex-priest: The process of leaving a high commitment status. *Sociological Inquiry*, 45, 41–49. Doi:10.1111/j.1475-682X.1975.tb00348.x.

Fernandez, E. R. (2001). Leaving the priesthood: A close reading of priestly departures. Ateneo University Press.

Fichter, S., J. (2009). When priests leave the church. Retrieved October 15, 2016 from http://www.americamagazine.org/issue/709/100/when-priests-leave-church

Greeley, A. (2004). For priests, celibacy is not a problem. Retrieved October 16, 1016 from http://www.nytimes.com/2004/03/03/opinion/for-priests-celibacy-is-not the-problem.html? pagewanted=all&src=pm

Guillen, F. (2009). The first five years of the priesthood. A study of newly ordained catholic priests. *Philippiniana Sacra, 44*(130), 227-228.

Hankle, D. (2010). The psychological processes of discerning the vocation to the catholic priesthood: A qualitative study. *Pastoral Psychology, 59*(2), 201-219.

Hickson, J. H., & Gudz, G. (1995). Group work with catholic priests who have exited the clerical world. *Counseling & Values, 40*(1), 32.

Hoge, D. R., & Okure, A. (2006). International priests in America: Challenges and opportunities. Liturgical Press.

Isacco, A., Sahker, E., Hamilton, D., Mannarino, M. B., Sim, W., & St Jean, M. (2014). A qualitative study of mental health help-seeking among catholic priests. *Mental Health, Religion & Culture, 17*(7), 741-757.

Kane, M. N. (2008). A qualitative survey of the attitudes of catholic priests toward bishops and ministry following the sexual abuse revelations of 2002. *Pastoral Psychology, 57*(3-4), 183-198.

Kennedy, E. C., Heckler, V. J., Kobler, F. J., & Walker, R. E. (1977). Clinical assessment of a profession: Roman catholic clergymen. *Journal of Clinical Psychology, 33*(1), 120-128.

Knox, S., Virginia, S. G., Thull, J., & Lombardo, J. P. (2005). Depression and contributors to vocational satisfaction in roman catholic secular clergy. *Pastoral Psychology, 54*(2), 139-155. Doi:10.1007/s11089-005-6199-1

Leaving the Priesthood. (n.d.). Leaving the priesthood. Retrieved October 16, 2016 from http://www.leavingthepriesthood.com/index.html

Leedy, P. & Ormrod, J. (2001). Practical research: Planning and design (7th ed.). Upper Saddle River, NJ: Merrill Prentice Hall. Thousand Oaks: SAGE Publications

Louque, M. (2006). Evolving visions of the priesthood: Changes from Vatican II to the turn of the century. *Catholic Education, (1)*, 106.

Mathers, N., Fox, N., & Hunn, A. (2007). Surveys and questionnaires. National institute for Health Research.

McLeod, S. A. (2007). Psychodynamic Approach. Retrieved from www.simplypsychology.org/psychodynamic.html

McLeod, S. A. (2014). Carl Rogers. Retrieved from www.simplypsychology.org/carl-rogers.html

McLeod, S. A. (2016). Maslow's Hierarchy of Needs. Retrieved from www.simplypsychology.org/maslow.html

Pietkiewicz, I. (2016). Reaching a decision to change vocation: A qualitative study of former priests' experiences. *International Journal for educational and vocational guidance, 16,* 379-404.

Pope, C. (2015). Leaving priesthood. Retrieved October 16, 2016 from https://www.osv.com/OSVNewsweekly/Article/TabId/535/ArtMID/13567/ArticleID/16803/Leaving-Priesthood.aspx

Rakosza, K. (2016). Why do priests resign from priesthood?. Retrieved October 16, 2016 from http://www.vice.com/read/why-do-priests-resign-from-priesthood-876

Rossetti, S.J. (2011). Why priests are happy: A study of the psychological and spiritual health of priests. *Publishers Weekly, 258*(37), 74.

Rossetti, S. J., & Rhoades, C. J. (2013). Burnout in catholic clergy: A predictive model using psychological and spiritual variables. *Psychology of Religion and Spirituality, 5*(4), 335.

Rulla, L. M., Ridick, J., & Imoda, F. (1976). Entering and leaving vocation: Intrapsychic dynamics. Gregorian Biblical BookShop.

Schallert, E. J., & Kelley, J. M. (1970). Some factors associated with voluntary withdrawal from the catholic priesthood. International Centre for Studies in Religious Education.

Schoenherr, R., & Greeley, A. (1974). Role commitment processes and the 44merican catholic priesthood. *American Sociological Review, 39*(3), 407-426. Retrieved from http://www.jstor.org/stable/2094298

Schoenherr, R. A., & Young, L. A. (1990). Quitting the clergy: Resignations in the roman catholic priesthood. *Journal for the Scientific Study of Religion, 4,* 463.

Schoenherr, R., & Young, L. (1993). Full pews and empty altars. *Journal of Economic Literature. 2.*

Shutz, D. (2007). Sentire cum ecclesia. Retrieved October 16, 2016 from https://scecclesia.wordpress.com/2007/10/15/more-damned-statistics-this-time-of priests-who-leave-the-priesthood-and-some-who-return/

Sunardi, Y. (2014). Predictive factors for commitment to the priestly vocation: A study of priests and seminarians. *Dissertations* (2009).

Umoren, L. (2006). The phenomenon of departure from congregation from a psychological point of view: Intrapsychic dynamics. *Vincentiana.*

Uy, (2013). PH catholic church badly needs priests for growing flock. Retrieved October 16, 2016 from http://newsinfo.inquirer.net/464305/ph-catholic-church-badly needs-priests-for-growing-flock

VandenBos, G. (2006). The APA dictionary of psychology. *American Psychological Association.*

Vatican Insider. (2014). Men who give up the priesthood for the love of a woman. Retrieved October 16, 2016 from http://www.lastampa.it/2014/05/19/vaticaninsider/eng/the-vatican/men-who-give-up-the-priesthood-for-the-love-of-a-woman tfGqnRvxYj2aduuyBsO3OJ/pagina.html

Verdieck, M. J., Shields, J. J., & Hoge, D. R. (1988). Role commitment processes revisited: American catholic priests 1970-1985. *Journal for the Scientific Study of Religion, 27*(4), 524-535.

Yalom, I. D. (1985). Theory and practice of group psychotherapy. Retrieved October 16, 2016 fromhttp://www.scirp.org/(S(oyulxb452alnt1aej1nfow45))/reference/ReferencesPapers.aspx?ReferenceID=1919444

ABOUT THE AUTHOR

*M*r. Christian Amaranto Semeniano obtained his Bachelor of Science in Psychology Degree at Ateneo de Naga University, cum laude. He has earned units in AB Philosophy at Holy Rosary Minor Seminary and took his certificate in professional teaching at University of Santo Tomas – Legazpi City. He is also a licensed Psychometrician.

He has conducted several researches and served as a research adviser since 2017. He also presented his undergraduate thesis during the 8th Joint Multidisciplinary Research Conference (JMRC), an international conference at Hotel Jen Manila, Pasay City, Philippines in 2018. He is being assessed for appropriate membership grade in the Royal Institute of Research Singapore by the Ascendens Asia. Moreover, his research abstract was published on Ascendens Asia Journal of Multidisciplinary Research Conference Proceedings.

Currently, he is taking his Master's Degree in Guidance and Counseling at Bicol University Graduate School. He is also a faculty member of St. Agnes Academy, Inc. as a research teacher in Senior High School.

E-mail: Christian.Semeniano08@Gmail.Com

www.ingramcontent.com/pod-product-compliance
Lightning Source LLC
Chambersburg PA
CBHW081252250726
48654CB00012B/1580